Compiled by Joan Frey Boytim

CONTENTS

The price of this publication includes access to companion recorded piano accompaniments online, for download or streaming.

Laura Ward, pianist
Larry Rock, engineer
Recorded May 2000, Settlement Music School, Germantown, Pennsylvania

ISBN 978-0-634-01971-5

G. SCHIRMER, *Inc.*

7777 W. BLUEMOUND RD. P.O. BOX 13819 MILWAUKEE, WI 53213

To access companion recorded piano accompaniments online, visit:
www.halleonard.com/mylibrary

Enter Code
5242-8504-3039-6512

PREFACE

Easy Songs for Beginning Singers will appeal to the middle school age group as well as to many beginning high school, college, and adult students. There are between 22 and 24 songs in each book with online accompaniments included.

Suitable vocal repertoire for the middle school student taking voice lessons has been rather sparse. For many years, most young people did not begin vocal study until the ninth or tenth grade level or even later. There was a misconception that it was a dangerous practice to study voice at an earlier age. As teachers have become more knowledgeable, as students are maturing much earlier, and as musicals are being produced in the middle schools, one finds many young people beginning lessons in the seventh and eighth grades and even earlier.

The foreign language texts have been purposely eliminated to make the songs very easy to learn. Modification has been made to the dated English versions and, in some cases, new texts have been provided. The songs are quite short and they generally have rather moderate tessituras. The maximum ranges, explored in only a few selections, are C to G for soprano, A to E for mezzo, C to F-sharp for tenor, and A-flat to E-flat for baritone. Most songs do not use those extended ranges.

A number of the songs will not be familiar but should prove to be a welcome addition to well known repertoire published in these collections. At the same time, I have included a few popular standards in each volume. Songs in the female books explore many folk songs and interesting translated French bergerettes and early German lieder. The male volumes each contain a number of English and American folksongs, spirituals, and several art songs. There are several quite humorous songs in each of the books.

Most of the accompaniments are suitable for student pianists. A few songs in each volume will be more of a challenge to lead the student directly into Schirmer's *First Book of Solos* and *First Book of Solos Part II.*

Birth and death dates for composers have been included whenever possible. These dates are simply not known for a few of the composers, particularly minor musical figures who had few published works. In lieu of birth and death dates, publication dates are provided, when known, to allow a teacher or student at least some chronological perspective for a song.

It is my hope that these four volumes will provide a new and worthwhile source of music for the novice singer of any age, as well as a fun collection for the more experienced student of voice.

Joan Frey Boytim

BIOGRAPHY

Compiler Joan Frey Boytim is a nationally recognized expert in teaching beginning voice students and has conducted workshops, seminars, and master classes across the United States. She is the compiler of the widely used series *The First Book of Solos, The First Book of Solos Part II, The Second Book of Solos,* and *The First Book of Broadway Solos*.

Come, Aurora

(Viens, Aurore)

Charles Fonteyn Manney

English, 16th century
arranged by O.H. Lange

The Ash Grove

English text by
John Oxenford

Welsh folksong

break - ing, A host of kind fa - ces is gaz - ing on me. The
friends of my child - hood a - gain are be - fore me, Each step wakes a
cresc.
mem - 'ry, as free - ly I roam, With soft whis - pers la - den, its
leaves rus - tle o'er me, The ash grove, the ash grove a - lone is my

home.
My
f
lips smile no more, my heart los - es its light - ness, No dream of the
p
fu - ture my spir - it can cheer; I on - ly would brood on the
past and its bright - ness, The dead I have mourned are a - gain liv - ing

here. From ev - 'ry dark nook they press for - ward to meet me, I
lift up my eyes to the broad leaf - y dome, And o - thers are
there look - ing down - wards to greet me, The ash grove, the ash grove a -
lone is my home.

By the Light of the Silvery Moon

moon.
core.
By the light
of the sil-ver-y
moon.
I want to
spoon,
To my hon-ey I'll
croon
love's
tune,
Hon-ey
moon
keep a-shin-ing in
June,
Your sil - v'ry
beams will bring love dreams, We'll be cud - dling
soon,
By the sil-ver-y
moon.
moon.
1.
2.

Drink to Me Only with Thine Eyes

Ben Jonson

old English air

I sent thee late a ros - y wreath, Not
pp
so _ much hon' - ring thee ___ As giv-ing it a hope that there It could not with - ered
be; ___ But thou there-on didst on - ly breathe And sent it back to me; ___
Since when it grows, and smells, I swear, Not of ___ it-self, but thee!
pp

A Fable
(Une Fable)

English text by
Edith Clegg

Anton Arensky
1861-1906

sf
snapped her up, for half a meal is bet-ter than none at all. Hmm,
hmm, is bet-ter than none at all.
p
poco meno mosso
Far up on high came
poco meno mosso
p
drift-ing by an ea-gle old and grim, he saw be-low the spar-row, so he
f
paused on out - spread wing.
p
The ea - gle too was hun - gry, he had
mf
p

killed no meat that day, With - out a sound, down to the ground, He
swooped up - on his prey! A hun - ter through the for - est was
riten.
Tempo I
ri - ding with his gun. He took his aim, the ea - gle fell! And so my sto - ry's
done, and so, and so my sto - ry's done!
rit.

Hark! Hark! the Lark

William Shakespeare

Franz Schubert
1797-1828

* The singer may choose to omit the interlude between verses.

chal - iced flow'rs that lies, On chal - iced flow'rs that
hope, till morn is nigh, And hope, till morn is
then wilt thou a - wake, O then wilt thou a -
lies. And wink - ing Ma - ry - buds be - gin To
nigh, That thou wilt wake, their light to greet: Come
wake! How Love thee to thy win - dow brings, Well
ope their gold - en eyes, With ev - 'ry thing that
ope thy star - ry eyes! Since thou so star - like
knows he: ope thine eyes, And love thy sing - er
pret - ty bin, My la - dy sweet, a - rise! With
art, so sweet, My la - dy sweet, a - rise! Since
while he sings! My la - dy sweet, a - rise! And

ev - 'ry thing that pret - ty bin, My la - dy sweet, a -
thou so star - like art, so sweet, My la - dy sweet, a -
love thy sing - er while he sings! My la - dy sweet, a -
f decresc.
rise! a - rise, a - rise, My
rise! a - rise, a - rise, My
rise! a - rise, a - rise, My
la - dy sweet, a - rise, a - rise, a -
la - dy sweet, a - rise, a - rise, a -
la - dy sweet, a - rise, a - rise, a -
1st and 2nd time D.S.
3rd time D.S. al Fine
rise, My la - dy sweet, a - rise!
rise, My la - dy sweet, a - rise!
rise, My la - dy sweet, a - rise!
p

Flow Gently, Sweet Afton

Robert Burns

James E. Spilman

dream. Thou stock - dove, whose ech - o re - sounds through the glen, Ye
wave. Flow gen - tly, sweet Af - ton, a - mong thy green braes, Flow
wild whis - tling black - birds in yon thorn - y den, Thou green - crest - ed
gen - tly, sweet riv - er, the theme of my lays; My Ma - ry's a -
lap - wing, thy scream - ing for - bear, I charge you dis - turb not my
sleep by thy mur - mur - ing stream, Flow gen - tly, sweet Af - ton, dis -
slum-ber-ing fair.
turb not her dream.

If You've Only Got a Moustache

Stephen C. Foster
1826-1864

mat - ter what may be your age, you al - ways may cut a fine dash. You will
take the ad - vice that I give; you'll soon gain af - fec - tion and cash and will
good friend, he gave me ad - vice and time - ly pre - vent - ed the splash; now at
suit all the girls to a hair if you've on - ly got a mous-tache, a mous -
be all the rage with the girls if you'll on - ly get a mous-tache, a mous -
home I've a wife and ten heirs, and all through a hand-some mous-tache, a mous -
tache, a mous - tache, if you've on - ly got a mous - tache.
tache, a mous - tache, if you'll on - ly get a mous - tache.
tache, a mous - tache, and all through a hand-some mous - tache.
8va
1.2.
3.
Your
I

I'm Always Chasing Rainbows

(based on "Fantasie-Impromptu" by Chopin)

Joseph McCarthy

Harry Carroll
1892-1962

Flowing

f

I'm al - ways chas - ing rain - bows, watch - ing clouds drift - ing by. My schemes are just like all my dreams, end - ing in the

sky.
Some fel-lows look and find the sun-shine, I
al-ways look and find the rain.
Some fel-lows make a win-ning some-time, I
nev-er e-ven make a gain. Be-lieve me, I'm
al-ways chas-ing rain-
bows,
wait-ing to find a lit-tle blue-bird in vain.
rit.
rit.

Katy Bell

George Cooper

Stephen C. Foster
1826-1864

The Little Irish Girl

Edward Teschmacher

Hermann Löhr
1871-1943

p quasi speech-like
f
tossed her pret-ty curl, "Well may - be I pre-fer it!" Och! the dear lit-tle girl!
colla voce
f
p
mf
mf
Says I, "Per-haps you're mar - ried?" Says
mf
she, "Per-haps I'm not." Says I, "I'll be your gos - soon!" Says she, "I'll not be caught." "Oh! your
mf
mf
quasi speech-like
f
p
eyes are like the o - cean, And your heart is like a pearl!" Says she, "Well then, I'll keep it." Och! the
f
p

p
dear lit - tle girl!
Says
f
I, "I've got a cab - in, And pigs that num - ber seven, And oh! with you Ma-vour-neen, Sure the
rall.
ten.
p
rall.
colla voce
place would be like heav'n!" Her_ eyes looked up in mine_then, My heart was in a whirl; The
mf
f
mf
lit - tle pigs had done it! Och! the dear_ lit - tle girl!
rall.
f

My Wild Irish Rose

Chauncey Olcott
1860-1932

giv - en to me by a girl that I know, Since we've met, faith I've known no re -
glan - ces are shy when - e'er I pass by, The bow - er where my true love
pose, She is dear - er by far than the world's bright - est star, And I
grows, And my one wish has been that some day I may win The
call her my wild I - rish Rose.
heart of my wild I - rish Rose.
My wild I - rish
p
Rose, the sweet - est flow'r that grows. You may

search ev - 'ry - where, but none can com - pare, With my wild I - rish
Rose. My wild I - rish Rose, The
dear - est flow'r that grows, And some day for my sake, she may let me
take, the bloom from my wild I - rish Rose. 2. They may Rose.
mf
rit.
rit.
1.
2.

Scarborough Fair

English folksong
arranged by Cecil J. Sharp
1859-1924

lov - er of mine.
lov - er of mine.
lov - er of mine.
2. Tell her to make me a cam - bric shirt, Pars - ley sage, rose - ma - ry and thyme, With - out a - ny nee - dle or thread worked in it, And she shall be a true lov - er of mine.
4. Tell her to plough me an a - cre of land, Pars - ley, sage, rose - ma - ry and thyme, Be - tween the sea and the salt sea strand, And she shall be a true lov - er of mine.
6. Tell her to reap it with a sick - le of leath - er, Pars - ley, sage, rose - ma - ry and thyme, And tie it all up with a tom - tit's feath - er, And she shall be a true lov - er of mine.
p
cresc.

7. Tell her to gath - er it all in a sack,
p
Pars - ley, sage, rose - ma - ry and thyme, And car - ry it home on a
but - ter - fly's back, And then she shall be a true lov - er of
mine.
dim.

Passing By

Edward Purcell
1689-1740
arranged by William Arms Fisher
1861-1948

rit.
a tempo
rit.
till I die.
till I die.
a tempo
mf
a tempo
Cu - pid is wing - ed and doth range Her coun - try, so my
a tempo
mp
love doth change, But change the earth or change the sky, Yet
con affetto
rit.
will I love her till I die.
rit.
pp

A Pretty Girl Is Like a Melody

text by the composer

Irving Berlin
1888-1989

like sun - ny weath - er goes with the month of May.
I've stud - ied girls and mu - sic, so I'm qual - i - fied to
say: A pret - ty girl is like a mel - o - dy
that haunts you night and day,

Just like the strain of a haunt - ing re -
frain, she'll start up - on a mar - a - thon and
run a-round your brain. You can't es - cape she's in your
mem - o - ry. By morn - ing, night and

noon
She will leave you and
then come back a - gain. A
1.
pret - ty girl is just like a pret - ty tune.
2.
A pret - ty tune.

Requiem
(™Underwoods∫)

Robert Louis Stevenson

Sidney Homer
1864-1953

p
grave for me: Here he lies where he longed to be;
p

mf cresc.
f
p
Home is the sail - or, home from sea, And the
mf cresc.
f

molto rit.
hunt - er home from the hill.
molto rit.
p

Rock-a-My-Soul

African-American spiritual
arranged by Cynthia Jackson

val - ley to pray, oh, rock - a - my soul, my soul got hap - py and I
val - ley at night, oh, rock - a - my soul, I knew that ev - 'ry - thing would
morn-ing be - fore, oh, rock - a - my soul, I found the peace that I was
cloud - i - est day, oh, rock - a - my soul, a prayer is all you need to
1.2.3.
4.
D.S. al Coda
stayed all day,
be al - right,
look - ing for,
light your way,
oh, rock - a - my soul. Oh, soul. Oh,
CODA
Oh! rock - a - my soul!

The Rose of Allandale

Charles Jeffry

Sydney Nelson
1800-1862
arranged by Walter Goodell

mf
flow - ers decked the moun - tain's side, And fra - grance filled the vale, By
tem - pests lashed our gal - lant bark, And rent her shiv - 'ring sail, One
mf
far the sweet - est flow - er there Was the Rose of Al - lan - dale.
maid - en form with - stood the storm: 'Twas the Rose of Al - lan - dale.
The
p
mf
f
Rose of Al - lan - dale, the Rose of Al - lan - dale, By
f
far the sweet - est flow-er there Was the Rose of Al - lan - dale.

The Rose of Tralee

C. Mordaunt Spencer

Charles W. Glover
1806-1863

più moto
lee; She was
lee; Though
love - ly and fair as the rose of the summer, Yet
più moto
'twas not her beau - ty a - lone that won me. Oh, no! 'twas the
rit.
a tempo
rit.
a tempo
p
truth in her eye ev - er dawn - ing, That made me love Ma - ry, The
Rose of Tra - lee.
1.
2.
The lee.
p

Santa Lucia

English text by
Theodore Marzials
Teodoro Cottrau
1827-1879

Slowly
p
1. See where the star of eve Beams gen - tly
2. See, see, how fair it is, There in mid -
p

yon - der, See where from wave to wave Soft breez - es wan - der! Far down the
o - cean, Rocked by the sil - ver waves With gen - tlest mo - tion. All sunk in

sil - ver track Twi - light is fall - ing, Far, oh! so far a - way,
peace and rest, All sweet - ly dream - ing, Now through the deep-'ning night

f piú moto
Sweet songs are call - ing. Come then, ere night is dark,
Moon - light is stream - ing. Come, then, ere night is o'er,
f piú moto
p
Come to my bound-ing bark, San - ta Lu - ci - a, San - ta Lu -
Come leave the nois - y shore, San - ta La - ci - a, San - ta Lu -
p
f
ci - a! Come, then, ere night is dark, Come to my
ci - a! Come, then, ere night is o'er, Come leave the
f
p
bound-ing bark, San - ta Lu - ci - a, San - ta Lu - ci - a!
nois - y shore, San - ta Lu - ci - a, San - ta Lu - ci - a!
p

Standin' in the Need of Prayer

African-American spiritual
arranged by Cynthia Jackson

me, O Lord, stand - in' in the need of
me, O Lord, stand - in' in the need of
prayer. Ain't my moth - er or my fa - ther, but it's me, O Lord,
prayer. Ain't my dea - con or my lead - er, but it's me, O Lord,
stand - in' in the need of prayer. Ain't my
stand - in' in the need of prayer. It's
1.
2.
D.S. al Coda
CODA
stand - in' in the need of prayer.

Steal Away

African-American spiritual
arranged by Cynthia Jackson

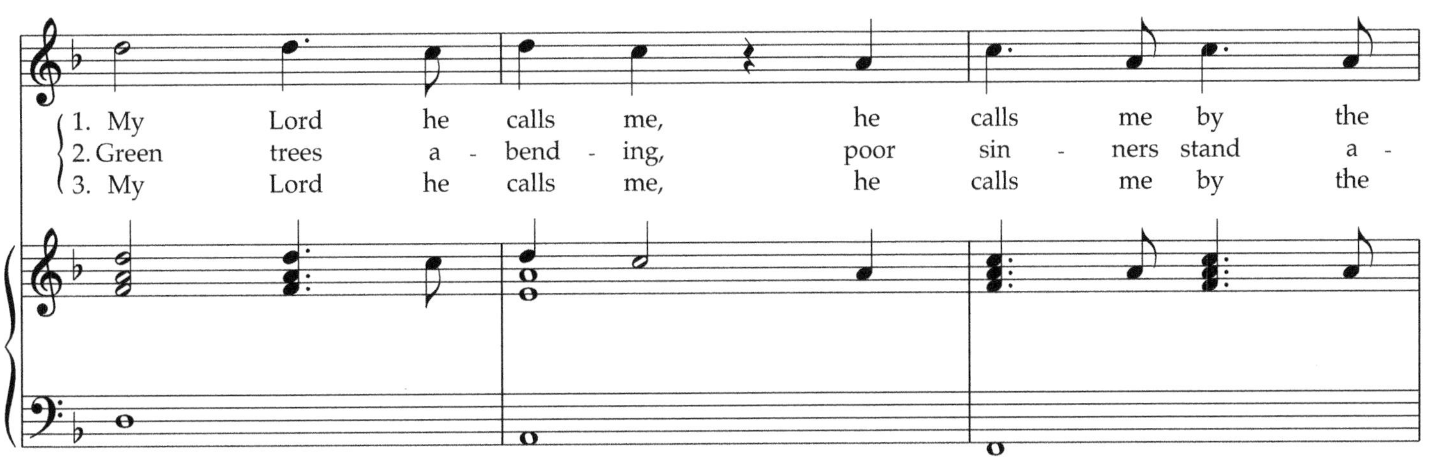
1. My Lord he calls me, he calls me by the
2. Green trees a - bend - ing, poor sin - ners stand a -
3. My Lord he calls me, he calls me by the

thunder;
trem - bling;
light - ning;
the trum - pet sounds with - in - a my soul. I
3

1.2.
3.
ain't got long to stay here. stay here.
8vb

When Irish Eyes Are Smiling

Chauncey Olcott and
George Graff, Jr.

Ernest R. Ball
1878-1927

sweet lilt - ing laugh - ter's like some love - ly song, And your eyes twink - le
spring - time of life is the sweet - est of all, There is ne'er a real
bright as can be;
care or re - gret;
ten.
You should laugh all the while and all
And while spring - time is ours through - out
ten.
oth - er times smile, And now smile a smile for me. When
all of youth's hours, Let us smile each chance we get. When
ten.
p
I - rish eyes are smi - ling, Sure it's like a morn in

Spring. In the lilt of I - rish laugh-ter, You can hear the
an - gels sing. When I - rish hearts are hap - py, All the
world seems bright and gay, And when I - rish eyes are smi -
mf
portamento
mf
p
ten.
ling, Sure they steal your heart a - way.
1.
2.
rit.
way.
ten.
p
f
rit.
rit.